Wedding
Decorations
on a Budget

Miriam Gourley

Sterling Publishing Co., Inc. New York
A Sterling/Chapelle Book

CHAPELLE LTD.

Owner
Jo Packham

Editor
Karmen Quinney

Staff
Areta Bingham • Kass Burchett • Marilyn Goff •
Holly Hollingsworth • Susan Jorgensen •
Barbara Milburn • Linda Orton • Leslie Ridenour •
Cindy Stoeckl • Gina Swapp • Sara Toliver

Photographers
Kevin Dilley/Hazen Photography Studio •
Scott Zimmerman

Library of Congress Cataloging-in-Publication Data

10 9 8 7 6 5 4 3 2 1

Published by Sterling Publishing Company, Inc.,
387 Park Avenue South, New York, NY 10016
© 2001 by Miriam Gourley
Distributed in Canada by Sterling Publishing
c/o Canadian Manda Group, One Atlantic Avenue, Suite
105 Toronto, Ontario, Canada M6K 3E7
Distributed in Great Britain and Europe by Cassell PLC
Wellington House, 125 Strand, London WC2R 0BB, England
Distributed in Australia by Capricorn Link (Australia) Pty Ltd.
P.O. Box 6651, Baulkham Hills, Business Centre, NSW 2153,
Australia
Printed in China
All Rights Reserved

Sterling ISBN 0-8069-5805-7

If you have any questions or comments, please contact:
Chapelle Ltd., Inc.,
P. O. Box 9252
Ogden, UT 84409
(801) 621-2777
FAX (801) 621-2788
e-mail:
Chapelle@chapelleltd.com
website: www.chapelleltd.com

A special thank you to Becky Miller, White Willow Reception-Provo, UT. Center; Laurel Cornia-Orem, Utah; Antia Louise Crane-Park City, Utah; Kathy Elliot-Bountiful, Utah; Mary Jo Hiney-Los Osos, CA; Chris Jarvis-Pleasant Grove, Utah; Shelia McDonald-Orem, Utah; and Jo Packham -Ogden, Utah; for allowing us to photograph parts of this book in their homes. Their trust and cooperation are greatly appreciated.

ABOUT THE AUTHOR

Miriam Gourley has been a professional designer for eighteen years. She works with fabric, stuffing, batting, embroidery floss, ribbons, beads, paints, wood, paper, and just about anything else which might be transformed into something beautiful for that special wedding celebration. Miriam feels that wedding decorations should be memorable, whether they are created from new materials or materials gathered up from your home, attic, or garden. These decorations can later be given as thank-yous to the wedding party or used to decorate your new home.

She has received a great deal of fulfillment in her career, and feels fortunate to be paid for something she loves to do.

We would like to offer our sincere appreciation for the valuable support given in this ever-changing industry of new ideas, concepts, designs, and products. Several items shown in this publications were created by the following: Ann Brinkley Designs 761 Palmer Ave. Holmdel, NJ 07733; Elements/Jill Schwartz 343 Main St. Great Barrington, MA 01230; Poco A Poco Imports, PO Box 9083, Berkley, CA 94709; and Stress Busters, 450 Bendale Rd. Severna Park, MD 21146. Several projects shown in this publication were created with the outstanding and innovative products developed by Americana Acrylic Paints, Delta Ceramcoat® Acrylic Paints, Hollywood Trims, Walnut Hollow, and Prym Dritz Corp.

Contents

Introduction

Every bride dreams of having a beautiful wedding that is the true essence of her romance. In this, the most romantic moment of her life, she wants to share in her own stylish way with everyone present the dreams of the past, the happiness of the day, and the hopes for tomorrow; all of which should be the very heart and soul of every wedding celebration.

Every bride has a style that she believes is the very spirit of who she is and what she loves. She envisions a wedding celebration that is the epitome of that style, that is perfect in every detail, and that has no limitations and no budgets.

No budgets—these are two words that usually are not written as part of the script for most bridal plans. Almost every bride must have a budget—so how does one have the wedding of her dreams with monetary restrictions and limitations?

For three wedding styles, one of which is perfect for almost any bride, the answers are here on the pages that follow.

Romantic Chic

"Come live with me, and be my love," said Ryne Hazen to his bride, Teresa, as they exchanged vows on a cloudless afternoon in May. From the days when Teresa was a little girl, she had dreamed of a romantic garden wedding—one with a long white dress, swans on the lake, and roses everywhere. To make her dream a day to remember forever, Teresa, her family, and all their friends offered their homes, their time, and their talents to make a truly romantic affair for this beautiful bride. The home and the gardens for the wedding were that of a friend, the food was prepared and served by both families, some of the decorations were borrowed, and some were made easily and inexpensively. The inspiration for each detail that made up this truly lovely afternoon came from all things of romance—roses that are blushingly tinted and forever unfading, remnants of plain cotton fabrics, lace that was delicately etched and aged, and simple time-worn objects with treasured imperfections and an innocent, comfortable appeal.

Teresa's dress was that which was worn by her mother on her wedding day. The swans that spent the afternoon swimming quietly in the sun were borrowed from the friend of a friend.

𝓔ntry Way

L a v i s h   C o l u m n s

Materials:

10' cardboard concrete forms

Bucket of sand

Construction adhesive

Craft paints–brown, gold,
gray, white

Embossed wallpaper border

Plastic urn with 8"-dia. bottom

Prewired light socket

Silk ivy garland

Unbleached muslin

Wallboard joint compound

Supplies:

Electric drill/1" drill bit

Paintbrushes–6" flat nylon, fan

Instructions:

1. Apply wallpaper border around top edge of concrete form, following manufacturer's instructions.

2. Drill 1" hole 2" up from bottom of concrete form. Drill 1" hole at base of urn.

3. Using your hands, texture entire concrete form with wallboard joint compound. *Make certain any lettering on concrete form is completely covered.*

4. Repeat Step 3 with urn. Allow to dry.

5. Using flat paintbrush and brushing vertically, randomly streak concrete form and urn with gray paint.

6. Streak gold over concrete form and urn, allowing some gray and white to show through.

7. Streak white over raised areas of texture. Allow to dry.

8. Using edge of fan brush, randomly make "crack lines" down sides of concrete form and urn and blend edges with diluted gray. Allow to dry.

9. Place prewired light socket down middle of urn and base.

10. Place urn on top of concrete form and thread plug and cord down through concrete form and through 1" hole drilled near bottom of concrete form. Pull snugly.

11. Set concrete form with urn in bucket of sand.

12. Apply construction adhesive to inner rim of urn base. Place urn at top of concrete form.

13. While construction adhesive is still wet, secure one end of silk ivy under base of urn. Allow to dry.

14. Randomly hot-glue ivy to concrete form.

15. Wrap bucket with muslin to hide cord and bucket. Plug in prewired light socket.

Fresh flowers can be picked from the garden and placed in urns with silk flowers whose beauty never fades.

14

MUSLIN-DRAPED CHAIRS

Materials:

Chair

Cream tulle

Unbleached muslin

Supplies:

Fabric scissors

Instructions:

1. Wash and dry muslin. Do not iron.

2. Drape fabric from floor, over back of chair, across seat, and down to floor. Cut away excess muslin.

3. Use length of tulle to tie around back of chair at base of seat. Tie tulle into large bow. Trim ends.

Weathered Wooden Pedestal

Materials:

Acrylic paints–lt. cream,
dk. gray, tan

Crackle medium

Small finish nails

Spray sealer

Wood (scraps)–1" x 4" x 14½" (4),
1" x 4" x 16½" (4),
¼" x 14" x 41" oak veneer panel (4),
2" x 4" x 41" pine (4),
1" x 6" x 17" (3)

Wood glue

Wood screws: 1¾"

Supplies:

Electric drill/1¾" drill bit

Extrafine sandpaper

Hammer

Paintbrush

Saw

Tape measure

Instructions:

1. Lay two pine 2" x 4" on 4" sides, parallel to each other, 13" apart. Place oak veneer panel on top of 2" x 4", lining up all edges.

2. Drill holes for wood screw in three places on each side. Screw panel to 2" x 4".

3. Repeat Step 2 for remaining 2" x 4" and panels.

4. Stand panels up on one side, parallel to each other, 13" apart. Place oak veneer panel on top of 2" x 4", lining up all edges.

5. Drill holes for wood screws. Screw panel in place. Turn over to opposite side and repeat, adding fourth panel.

6. Measure lower edge and cut one 1" x 4" piece to fit. Screw in place at corners. *Make certain not to drill into previous screws, which are underneath.*

7. Repeat Step 6 for upper edge, then turn to opposite side and repeat.

8. Measure two remaining sides, top, and bottom edges. Attach 1" x 4" pieces to finish top and bottom edges.

9. Measure length between top and bottom borders. Apply wood glue to one corner molding. Tack molding in place with nails. Repeat for remaining three corners.

10. Center and place three pieces 1" x 6" x 17" over top of stand. Drill holes for screws in each corner. Screw top in place.

11. Sand edges to smooth.

12. Paint pedestal top with dk. gray paint. Paint lower pedestal with tan paint.

13. Apply crackle medium to pedestal, following manufacturer's instructions.

14. Paint over crackle medium with lt. cream paint. Allow to dry.

15. Spray with sealer.

This pedestal was made with scraps left over from a remodeling job. Visit your local lumber store and find scrap lumber sometimes for a nominal fee—sometimes free—or visit construction sites and ask (don't just take) to see their scrap pile. Adapt the size to whatever you can find.

$\mathcal{S}$ ign In Table

FRINGED TABLE DRAPING

Materials:

Cording

Fabrics–(to cover round table),
(to create scarf topper)

Fringe trim

Supplies:

Fabric scissors

Helping hand

Pencil

Sewing machine/zipper foot

Straight pins

String

Tape measure

Measuring Hints

*Measure the distance from the floor to the center of the table you wish to cover, adding 2"–3" if you wish to have it puddle on the floor (**Measurement A**). Multiply this number by four to determine yardage.*

Most fabric is 45" or 60" wide. You will probably only be able to cut one half-circle from one width of fabric, depending on the width of the fabric.

Divide the final number by 36 to determine the number of yards to purchase. It is a good idea to add an extra ⅓ yard, in case some extra fabric is needed.

Instructions:

1. Cut "Measurement A" plus 2" of fabric. Cut length of string to "Measurement A." Make small knot in one end and tie remaining end of string to pencil.

2. Open up piece of fabric on flat hard work surface. Place pencil on one selvage edge of fabric.

3. Have your helping hand hold knotted end along center of selvage fabric so that string is fairly taut.

4. Without moving knot, draw half-circle on fabric. See Diagram A. Continue to hold string taut as you mark circular shape.

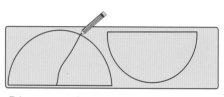

Diagram A

5. Cut out half-circle. Pin half-circle onto next piece of fabric. Using half-circle as a pattern, cut out second half-circle. See Diagram B.

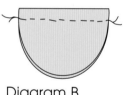

Diagram B

6. Using sewing machine and with right sides together and leaving ¼" seam allowance, machine-stitch center seam to form circle. Press seam open. *A French seam or serger can be used to create this seam.*

7. Using sewing machine, zigzag-stitch raw edge of table covering. Set aside.

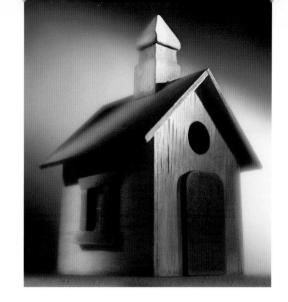

8. Measure width and length of fabric for table scarf. See Measuring Hints on facing page. *Make certain to trim off selvage edges before measuring if they do not match rest of fabric.* Cut fabric into a square.

9. Zigzag-stitch raw edges and set aside.

10. See Cording and Fringe Hints at right. Place flat woven edge of cording on right side of table cover's zigzagged edge. Using zipper foot, stitch cording onto table cover.

11. Press seam allowances toward wrong side of table cover, placing cording on outside edge. Blind-stitch raw edges to inside of table cover.

12. Repeat Steps 10–11 for scarf fabric, cording and fringe trim.

Cording and Fringe Hints

When stitching large-sized cording, unravel the beginning and end of cording to flatten. When reaching a corner, clip flat edge, just up to cording or fringe, to assist in making neat, angular corners.

A table cover that can be used in the future, a vintage copy of favorite sonnets, and flowers from the garden are perfect accessories for the guest book table at a romantic wedding.

EMBOSSED SWEETHEART'S FRAME

Materials:

⅛" foam-core board (scrap)

Craft glue

Doubled cord/tassels (optional)

Embossed wallpaper

Felt (to cover back of frame)

Matte spray sealer

Oak gel stain

Photograph

Taupe acrylic paint

Trim (scrap)

Unfinished rectangular or square
pine frame

Supplies:

1" sponge brush

Craft knife

Craft stick

Flat paintbrush

Fine-grit sanding pad

Paper towels

Instructions:

1. Lightly sand frame to prepare surface. Using paper towels, wipe frame. Lightly spray sealer on frame.

2. Using craft stick, apply glue to top of frame, covering entire surface up to edges.

3. With right side up, place wallpaper on glued surface. Smooth wallpaper to remove any air bubbles. When wallpaper begins to hold in place, turn frame upside down. Allow to dry for at least 30 minutes.

4. Trim wallpaper, leaving 1" below bottom edge of frame.

5. Fold wallpaper over top and bottom edges of frame. Apply small amount of glue to corner and continue gluing top and bottom edges of wallpaper so they fold around sides at corner.

6. Fold excess, overlapping onto back side of frame, apply glue and hold edges in place for a few seconds. Repeat for sides.

7. Trim off excess paper to fit edge of inside opening.

8. Paint papered area with taupe paint. Allow to dry. If necessary, apply second coat. Allow to dry.

9. Using sponge brush, apply gel stain to frame one section at a time, following manufacturer's instructions. Using paper towel, remove excess gel stain.

10. Spray frame with sealer.

11. Glue trim around opening on front of frame.

12. Cut piece of foam-core board to fit snugly inside picture opening.

13. Set photograph inside opening. Place foam-core board at back of opening to support photograph.

14. Cut felt to fit back of frame.

15. Apply glue to back of frame. Press felt onto glue. Allow to dry.

A hanger can be made by stapling a doubled cord with tassels on the end to the back of picture frame, leaving a loop at top for hanging.

Instructions:

1. Using vinegar and clean rag, wipe surface of vase.

2. Dip handle end of paintbrush into paint and make one to three dots. Repeat as desired.

Some glass paints are dishwasher-proof after you "cure" them in an oven for approximately 30 minutes at 200° Fahrenheit.

ADORNED GLASS VASE

Materials:

Clear glass vase

White glass paint

Supplies:

Clean rag

Small paintbrush

Vinegar

There are so many elements that inspire you to create the perfect details for a Romantic Chic wedding. Items that are seen and used everyday take on an appealing simplicity when used as decorations for a special day. Clay pots painted buttercup yellow with candles and flowers from the garden, picnic tinware used as *a wonderful* bowl for floating candles, and a *glass cylinder* filled with nuts and topped *with a moss* topiary ball are unconventional, unexpected, and mis-matched but delicate, familiar, and now treasured.

CANDLELIT BLOSSOMS

Instructions:

1. Wash grapes and set aside to dry.

2. Fill each vial with water mixture and replace rubber top.

3. Cut rose stems at an angle to 6"–8" in length. Push stems into vials until immersed.

4. Place wreath in center of table. Trim ends of greenery to 6"–8" in length. Push stems into vials until immersed.

Materials:

18"-dia. silk evergreen wreath

Candle

Candleholder

Floral water vials/rubber tops

Fresh flowers–cream roses, feverfew, white daisies, white lavender

Fresh greenery–fern fronds, lemon leaves

Red grapes (3–5 clusters)

Water mixed with floral preservative

Supplies:

Craft knife

5. Randomly insert greenery then roses into wreath, making certain vials cannot be seen.

6. Trim remaining flowers as necessary. Insert flowers into wreath.

7. Place grapes carefully around wreath with pointed ends of clusters draping over outside edge of wreath.

8. Place candleholder and candle in center of wreath.

Light candle when guests arrive. Watch candles carefully, they may need to replaced from time to time.

SHELL-CIRCLED TOPIARY

Instructions:

1. Paint entire pot with cream paint. Allow to dry. Apply second coat of paint. Allow to dry. Spray with sealer.

2. Apply craft glue to topiary base. Press moss onto glue, molding to fit shape of base. *If necessary, secure moss with T-pin while drying.*

3. Apply glue to top section. Repeat Step 2.

4. Firmly press topiary into pot. Adhere seashells around top border of pot.

Materials:

16" foam topiary base

Cream acrylic paint

Gloss spray sealer

Moss

Seashells

Small terra-cotta pot (to fit topiary base)

White craft glue

Supplies:

Flat paintbrush

Floral T-pins (optional)

Hot-glue gun

FAUX WEDDING CAKE

Materials:

Acrylic paints–cream, lt. yellow

Acrylic modeling compound

Glass cake stand

Matte spray sealer

Round papier-mâché hat box
(to fit on cake stand)

Supplies:

Cake-decorating kit

Craft scissors

Disposable cake-decorating
bag

Flat paintbrush

Instructions:

1. Paint inside and outside of box and lid with cream paint. Allow to dry. Repeat two times. Allow to dry. Spray inside and outside of box and lid with sealer.

2. Mix five parts modeling compound with one part lt. yellow paint, making certain mixture is blended well.

3. Place coupler in end of bag. *If end of bag is too small, clip off small pieces until coupler threads are outside bag.*

4. Attach desired small decorating tip for border onto end of coupler.

5. Place mixture into decorating bag. Push mixture into tip of bag, being careful not to let mixture ooze out top. Twist decorating bag close to mixture. Practice desired border on scrap of paper before applying to box.

6. Create border on box, making certain not to touch border to cake stand. Allow to dry for 4–12 hours, depending on humidity.

A bouquet of fresh flowers or a statue can be added to top of cake.

When planning a garden wedding on a budget, dress the flower girls in simple summer dresses of soft aqua and bare feet and have them carry baskets full of freshly picked flowers.

PAPER-COVERED VASE

Materials:

Acrylic paints–dk. brown, lt. gold, sand

Acrylic paint extender

Brown wrapping paper

Cylindrical glass vase

Heavy jute twine

White craft glue

Supplies:

Craft scissors

Gallon bucket

Instructions:

1. Fill bucket with tepid water.

2. Tear small pieces from brown paper, crinkle pieces into balls, and drop into bucket.

3. Remove paper balls from bucket and squeeze out excess water. Working in one small area at a time, apply craft glue to outside of vase. Smooth paper over glued areas on vase.

4. Repeat Steps 2–3 until entire surface is covered. *A small amount of glue may need to be applied to edges of paper to secure.* Allow to dry.

5. Mix five parts paint extender and one part dk. brown acrylic paint. Apply mixture over paper. *Do not worry about being perfectly even, or getting paint in every little crack.* Allow to dry.

6. Repeat Step 5 with lt. gold paint then repeat with sand paint. *The layers of paint will build over each other, giving wonderful depth to the vase.* Allow to dry between coats.

7. Spray with sealer.

8. Trim top edge even with top of vase. Wrap twine around vase three times. Tie in a square knot. Trim ends to about 1½". Fray cut ends of twine.

Candlelight is always a necessary part of any Romantic Chic wedding. These silver-toned candlesticks were purchased on a closeout at a discount store and the unattractive glass shades were covered with fabric remnants or pieces of lace. Each shade can be different, so have several friends create several different shades—it will be a tender touch of soft light as delicate as the first breeze of spring.

31

Vintage Chic

On an extraordinary summer afternoon in early June, the wedding day of Sara Buehler and Brett Toliver, the dreams of a young girl who wished for a Cinderella wedding came true. In her heart she knew the kind of bride she wanted to be, what she would wear, and what kind of wedding she would have. It would have moments of grandeur surrounded by that which was well-worn with years of love. If there was to be something new enjoyed during this wedding day, it must be made to look old and have the beauty of being imperfect . . . yet simple and well-loved.

It was a wedding in which Sara drew on tradition and personal style to create the perfect expression of her own joy and hope. It is these moments that will be forever savored, making the memories as beautiful as the dreams.

Sparklers lit up the summer night like tiny fireflies, sending the bride and groom into their tomorrows.

All of the fashions, furnishings, and keepsakes at Sara's and Brett's wedding were the essence of what has come to be recognized as a Shabby Chic Style. That which is elegant yet simple, worn yet well-loved, mismatched yet perfect together.

BOOK TABLE & ENTRY

After the wedding ceremony performed at the church that sits at the end of a country lane, the members of the wedding walked across the meadows to the home of an aunt who had adored Sara all of her life. The summer porches and the gardens had been tended and decorated with loving hands. Everywhere could be seen the dilapidated elegance of once-grand touches and the worn grandeur of faded fabrics and mismatched garden flowers. The candle pillars up the short stairway to the guest book table were made from weathered lumber, discarded balusters, and pieces of rusted tin. The potted plants from the garden were used in place of florist ones, and the candles were lit for the coming evening hours. The guest book was a scrapbook that had been made from the prettiest things in Aunt Linda's scrap box—even the candle snuffer is odd pieces of wire and two lone beads, found at the bottom of a box. Each detail on the table was delicate, handmade, and placed just so to capture each guest's heart.

CRACKLED-CANDLE PILLARS

Materials:

Baluster

Candles (3)

Crackle medium

Nails

Rusted tin

White acrylic paint

Wood–4" x 4" x 3" (2),
10" x 10" x 1" (3)

Supplies:

Hammer

Saw

Tin snips

Instructions:

1. Cut both 4" x 4"s to desired lengths for candleholders.

2. Apply crackle medium to wood pieces and baluster, following manufacturer's instructions.

3. Using tin snips, cut three tin pieces ¼" larger all around than bottom of candle. *Decorative designs can be cut into tin pieces if desired.*

4. Center and nail one tin piece to one end of 4" x 4". Repeat for remaining 4" x 4" and baluster.

5. Center and nail remaining ends of 4" x 4"s and baluster to wooden squares.

6. Place candles on top of candle-holders.

CHARMING CRACKLED CANDLE

Instructions:

1. Adhere charms onto candle with clear silicone, following manufacturer's instructions. Allow to dry overnight.

2. Using flat paintbrush, apply acrylic gesso to sides of pillar candle and charm. *Several coats may be necessary to provide full coverage. Make certain no acrylic gesso gets on top of candle where burning occurs.*

3. Mix off-white acrylic paint with first step of mosaic crackle medium. Determine ratio of paint to medium, following manufacturer's instructions. Paint mixture onto candle sides. Allow to dry for 30 minutes.

4. Paint over candle sides with mosaic crackle activator. *If work area is cool, cracking may take more time.*

5. Using rag, rub antiquing medium over candle sides.

6. Burn candle down just enough to place a tea light candle in top for burning.

Materials:

Acrylic gesso

Antiquing medium

Charms

Clear silicone

Off-white acrylic paint

Pillar candle

Tea light candle

Two-step mosaic crackle medium /activator

Supplies:

Clean rag

Flat paintbrush

BUCKET BOUQUET

Instructions:

1. Wash bucket with vinegar. Using paper towels, dry bucket.

2. Spray bucket with paint, following manufacturer's instructions. Allow to dry for 24 hours.

3. Decide where motifs will be placed on bucket. Using sponge brush, apply decoupage medium onto bucket. Place motifs on bucket. Using fingers, smooth out any wrinkles or air bubbles.

4. Apply decoupage medium over motifs. Allow to dry.

5. Apply decoupage medium over entire bucket. Allow to dry for 24 hours.

6. Apply antiquing medium, following manufacturer's instructions. Using rag, remove excess antique medium. Allow to dry.

7. Spray with varnish.

Materials:

Antiquing medium

Bucket

Decoupage medium

Spray paint

Spray varnish

Wallpaper or wrapping paper motifs

Supplies:

1" sponge brush

Clean rag

Paper towels

Vinegar

RUSTIC RECEPTION DECOR

Materials:

Acrylic paints–metallic gold, blue-green, metallic pewter, rust, white

Ceramic bird on steel post

Extrafine sand

Liquid dish soap

Matte finish decoupage medium

Medium-grit sandpaper

Terra-cotta pots

Two-step rusting agent

Supplies:

1" flat china-bristle paintbrush

Craft sticks

Disposable cup

Disposable plate

Eyedropper

Newspaper

Paper towels

Rubbing alcohol

Instructions:

1. Clean surface of bird and pots with dish soap in tub of hot water. Allow to dry.

2. Using paper towel soaked with rubbing alcohol, wipe outer surface of bird and pots, making certain to clean all crevices and detailed areas. Allow to dry.

3. Sand bird and pots. Using paper towel soaked with rubbing alcohol, wipe bird and pots.

4. Using craft stick and disposable cup, mix two parts decoupage medium with one part water. Mix well.

5. Paint over bird and pots with mixture for primer. Allow to dry.

6. Using craft stick and disposable cup, mix ¼ cup sand, one tablespoon decoupage medium, and two tablespoons white paint. Mix well.

7. Paint one coat of mixture over surfaces to be rusted.

8. Using craft stick and disposable plate, mix equal parts metallic gold and metallic pewter paints. Mix well.

9. Working vertically, paint over textured surfaces with mixture.

10. Paint streaks over metallic paint, before it dries, with blue-green and rust paints. Allow to dry.

11. Using newspaper, cover work surface to protect it from runs and drips.

12. Using eyedropper, apply two-step rusting agent to bird and pots, following manufacturer's instructions. Allow to dry 24 hours.

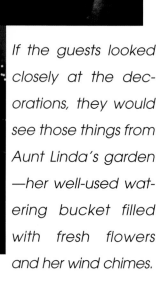

If the guests looked closely at the decorations, they would see those things from Aunt Linda's garden —her well-used watering bucket filled with fresh flowers and her wind chimes.

These delicate china mosaic wind chimes were made by artisan Becky Edwards. Even these have something old—pieces of grandmother's silver and something new—tiny charms that Sara chose.

Stained-glass windows salvaged from an old church hang on the porch to filter the afternoon sun, which makes prisms that dance on the flower petals.

EMBELLISHED GUEST BOOK

Instructions:

1. Measure width, height, and width of spine of scrapbook.

2. Use the following formula to determine outside dimensions for back cover:

width + spine + 2"

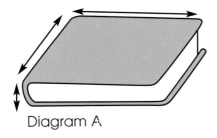

Diagram A

= back of cover width. Cut out one piece from needlepoint fabric to these dimensions for width x height plus 1". See Diagram A.

3. Using sewing machine, stitch velvet strips onto edges of needlepoint fabric for front of cover. Finished dimensions should be width plus 2" x height plus 1".

4. Cut two pieces one-third the width plus 1" x height plus 1" for inside flaps.

5. With right sides together, stitch back of cover to front of cover.

6. Fold one side flap under ½" and press. Repeat with remaining flap.

7. With right sides together, pin flaps to sides of cover. Stitch flaps together. See Diagram B. Turn right side out.

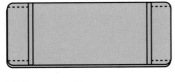

Diagram B

8. Fold top and bottom of cover in ½". See Diagram C. Press and stitch in place.

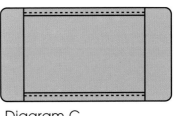

Diagram C

9. Slide book cover into ends. Pin lace to spine of book. Tack lace in place.

10. Tack tassel cord to back of cover and wrap tassel around large button for closure.

Materials:

Assorted buttons

Fabrics–needlepoint or decorative, velvet

Matching thread

Rectangular or square lace doily

Scrapbook

Tassel with cord

Supplies:

Fabric scissors

Iron/ironing board

Sewing machine

Sewing needle

Straight pins

Tape measure

LUMINOUS CANDLEHOLDER

Materials:

Candle taller than lamp shade

Candleholder

Lamp shade

Small seashells

Instructions:

1. Turn lamp shade upside down. Place in center of candleholder. Place candle inside lamp shade.

2. Place seashells around shade.

CUPID'S ARROW

The tiny treasures that are placed beside the guest book are each to honor romance and celebrate old friendships. The cupid's arrow was purchased during the engagement trip to Laguna Beach. It was made by an unknown artisan whose gentle inscription touched the hearts of both the bride and the groom. The tiny shell cases were bought the same day and filled with a wish for each from the other.

WEDDING PHOTO SHEATH

Materials:

8" x 12" cover stock

Photograph

Premade embossed photo mat
/photo corners

Supplies:

Craft glue

Craft knife

Paper scissors

Pen

Photocopy machine

Instructions:

1. Photocopy and enlarge Envelope Pattern on opposite page. Using paper scissors, cut out pattern. Trace pattern onto cover stock.

2. Cut out envelope. Using craft knife, lightly score envelope as marked on pattern. Cut slit as marked on pattern. Fold on scored lines.

3. Center and glue photo mat onto inside center section of envelope.

4. Secure photograph into photo corners.

Bride's & Groom's Table

Every wedding must have a place of honor for the bride and the groom. A table that is overflowing with those treasures that will become, from this day forward, the heirlooms of tomorrow. The keepsakes need not be expensive or new—handmade or given with love is all that is required. The dishes are Aunt Linda's picnic tinware with silver chargers placed underneath for a touch of elegance. Each has a box upon their plate with wishes written for a lifetime of happy tomorrows.

KEEPSAKE BOX

Materials:

Box/lid

Craft glue

Lace doily

Fabric–lace (to cover entire box), satin (to cover entire box)

Ribbon

Supplies:

Fabric scissors

Instructions:

1. Cut satin fabric to fit box. Repeat with lace fabric.

2. With wrong side of satin fabric facing up, center box on fabric. Glue fabric onto box. Repeat with lace fabric.

3. Repeat Steps 1–2 for lid.

4. Cut two lengths of ribbon long enough to wrap around box. Tie each length into a bow. Glue ribbons onto top of box and lid.

5. Apply small amount of glue on each corner of lid. Center doily on lid. Press doily down in each corner.

WEDDING FRAME

Materials:

Flat wooden frame

Seashells

Tacky craft glue

Supplies:

Craft stick

Instructions:

1. Using craft stick, apply glue to small section of frame. Press seashells into glue.

2. Continue until entire surface and edges are covered.

This tiny round basket was made especially for the groom. It is topped with a tiny shell lined in silver that was purchased the day he proposed and carries a wish from his bride for a lifetime of love and happiness.

Tiny glazed pots were filled with silk roses that are blushingly tinted and forever unfading. Lightly perched on the edge of the largest rose petal is a tiny china bird—a symbol of love's freedom.

The delicate heart box placed upon the bride's plate is filled with a wish from her groom for a lifetime of memories that honors both love and romance.

HEART BOX

Materials:

Decoupage medium

Gold leafing adhesive

Heart-shaped papier-mâché box

Leaf skeleton

Off-white acrylic paint

Supplies:

Glue brush

Paintbrush

Instructions:

1. Using paintbrush, paint box and lid. Allow to dry.

2. Apply gold leafing adhesive, following manufacturer's instructions.

3. Press gold leafing to adhesive.

4. Trim leaf to fit top of lid. Using glue brush, apply decoupage medium to leaf and place on lid. Apply another coat of decoupage medium. Allow to dry.

arents' Table

Second only in importance to the bride and groom are the parents of each. They are to be honored and thanked for not only all they have done on this day but for a lifetime of memories and dreams come true.

The parents' dining table must also be one that is designed to capture these dear ones' hearts. The toasting goblets are each different and meant to be the parents' gift of thank you. The glass bottles hold thank-yous, thoughtfully written by both bride and groom. The plates are mother-of-pearl and the chargers are, again, Aunt Linda's picnic tinware. The napkin rings are beaded, the flowers are created from painted pieces of old tin, and the chairs are wrapped in faded fabrics to match the fabric tablecloths.

It is at this table that memories will be remembered, stories will be told, and toasts to tomorrow will be made.

GLITTERING CANDLE VASE

Materials:

Acrylic modeling paste

Acrylic paint (to match wallpaper)

Glass cylinder vase

Glitter

Pillar candle

Reverse decoupage glue

Wallpaper (scrap)

Supplies:

Clean rag

Craft scissors

Cake-decorating kit/#13 decorating tip

Disposable cake-decorating bag

Flat paintbrush

Liquid dish soap

Instructions:

1. Clean and dry vase.

2. Cut wallpaper to fit inside of vase.

3. Using paintbrush, spread thin coat of reverse decoupage glue to front of wallpaper. Apply wallpaper to inside of vase.

4. Mix one-half jar of modeling paste with acrylic paint to match wallpaper.

5. Place coupler in end of bag. *If the end of the bag is too small, clip off small pieces until coupler threads are just inside bag.*

6. Attach #13 decorating tip for border onto end of coupler.

7. Place mixture into decorating bag, filling one-third of the way. Push mixture into tip of bag, being careful not to let mixture ooze out the top. Twist decorating bag close to mixture. Practice name and phrase on scrap of paper before applying to vase.

8. Write name and phrase on vase. See photograph on facing page.

9. Immediately sprinkle glitter over modeling paste. Allow to dry overnight.

10. Place pillar candle in vase.

BUTTERFLY NAPKIN RING

Materials:

11/0 seed beads–
blue-green, navy,
cascade green (one
container of each)

8/0 seed beads–blue,
dk. green
(one container of each)

6mm flat beads–cobalt blue
(2)

8mm round bead–jade

12mm x 8mm twisted
bead–turquoise blue

24-gauge silver wire

32-gauge silver wire

4mm silk ribbon (1 yd.)

Napkin ring

Supplies:

Florist tape

Needle-nosed pliers

Straight pin

Wire cutters

Instructions:

1. Using wire cutters, cut 24-gauge wire into two 30" lengths.

2. Slide 40 dk. green seed beads onto one length of wire. Move beads to center of wire and bend wire, forming loop. Twist wires together and bend loop into butterfly wing shape. Using needle-nosed pliers, tighten twists.

3. Repeat Step 2 for remaining upper wing, but do not twist two wings together. *The upper wings must be "filled" before they are joined.*

4. Cut 32-gauge wire into two 15" lengths.

5. Working with one wing at a time, tie one end of one length of wire to narrowest part of wing. Tightly drape wire along back side of wing so it is between first and second seed beads along lower edge of wing. Wrap wire between beads once.

6. Row 1: Slide one navy seed bead onto wire. Extend wire to top edge of wing and wrap it around anchor wire between first and second seed beads once.

7. Working from top wing edge, tightly drape wire along back side of wing so it is between second and third seed beads. Wrap wire between beads once.

8. Row 2: Slide three navy seed beads onto wire. Extend wire to bottom edge of wing and wrap it around anchor wire between third and fourth seed beads once.

9. Working from bottom wing edge, tightly drape wire along back side of wing so it is between third and fourth seed beads. Wrap wire between beads once.

10. Row 3: Slide four navy seed beads onto wire. Extend wire to top edge of wing and wrap it around anchor wire between third and fourth seed beads once.

11. Continue filling wing with navy seed beads in same manner (16 rows are needed to fill upper wing).

12. Wrap 32-gauge wire in between two anchor wire beads, then trim away excess wire. Tuck wire ends in between beads with straight pin.

13. Repeat Steps 2–9 for remaining upper wing.

14. Twist two upper wings together. Using needle-nosed pliers, tighten twists.

15. Working with wires from upper wings, bend two wires upward. They should extend to left and right of each other. Bend remaining two wires downward.

16. Working with wire on left, slide 31 blue seed beads onto wire. Bend wire to form loop and twist loop to anchor wing.

17. Repeat Step 16 for wire on right.

18. Cut 32-gauge wire in between two anchor wire beads. Trim away excess wire. Using straight pin, tuck wire ends in between beads.

19. Repeat Steps 5–18 for remaining upper wing.

20. Twist two lower wings together. Using needle-nosed pliers, tighten twists. Shape upper and lower wings.

21. Bend wires on lower wings upward to center back of butterfly, then bend them downward over center front of

butterfly. At this time, do nothing with wires from upper wings.

22. Slide jade round bead and turquoise blue twisted bead onto both wires. Separate wires and slide 13 navy seed beads onto each wire. Bend wires to back of twisted bead and upward toward upper wings on back side of butterfly.

23. Twist wires together then around center of butterfly to anchor wires. Twist wires together and bend them downward. Wrap twisted wires with florist tape and silk ribbon.

24. Working with one of the wires from upper wings, slide nine blue-green and nine cascade green seed beads onto wire, alternating colors. Slide cobalt blue flat bead and one cascade green seed bead onto wire. Slide beads down wire to meet round bead.

25. Using needle-nosed pliers and holding beads snugly together, tightly coil wire end several times. Flatten coil against uppermost seed beads. Using wire cutters, trim away excess wire.

26. Repeat Steps 1 and 2 for remaining wire.

27. Hot-glue butterfly onto desired napkin ring.

MESSAGE IN A BOTTLE

Write a message for your parents. Roll paper, tie with ribbon, and place into a bottle. Glue a polished piece of glass to the cork, creating a stopper.

Wedding Party's Table

The bridesmaids, the groomsmen, the flower girl, and the ring bearer all need to be seated in places of honor. These, after all, are the family and friends which you hold closest to your hearts. Their table is not covered in lace, but is overlapped and draped in vintage cabbage-rose cottons with frayed edges. There need be no sewing with these table linens—they are what they are—remnants of antique textiles, tapestries, trims, laces, and doilies. The chair backs for the men are adorned with strung shells and the women's have crocheted ribbon garlands with sachet hearts. Even the "candelabra" in the table's center is made from a glass dome and a garden vase. Everyday things made special.

FLORAL CHAIR CUSHION

Materials:

½"–1"-dia. buttons (4)

Floral fabric (2 yds.)

Pillow forms (2)

Supplies:

Fabric scissors

Sewing machine

Tape measure

Instructions:

1. Cut fabric for pillow bottom 3" larger than length and width of pillow form.

2. Cut Section A for pillow top to same length and two-thirds the width of bottom fabric measurement + 2½" for button overlap.

3. Cut Section B for pillow top to same length and one-third the width of bottom fabric measurement + 2½" for button placement.

4. Fold one edge of Section A's length in ½" and press. Fold in again

66

2" and press. Stitch along edge to finish. Mark and place button holes in fabric. See Diagram A.

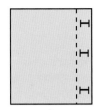

Diagram A

5. Fold one edge of Section B's length in ½" and press. Fold in again 1" and press. Stitch along edge to finish.

6. Place Section A button holes over finished edge of Section B, overlapping 1". Baste-stitch top and bottom edges. Mark and stitch buttons to bottom piece. See Diagram B. Overall size of top sections and bottom piece should be equal.

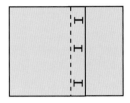

Diagram B

7. With right sides together, stitch around top and bottom pieces, leaving ½" seam allowance.

8. Pinch seams of one corner together separating top and bottom pieces. See Diagram C. Stitch across seam at 90° angle, 1" down from corner. See Diagram C. Repeat for all corners. Turn right side out. Press.

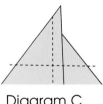

Diagram C

9. Insert pillow form, then button to close.

WRAPPED WITH A BOW

Materials:

Fabric (¼ yd.)

Floral wire

Matching thread

Pipe cleaners (2)

Supplies:

Fabric scissors

Iron/ironing board

Sewing machine

Sewing needle

Instructions:

1. Cut out two 9" x 16" rectangles.

2. Using sewing machine, stitch ½" seam around outside edge of rectangles, with right sides together, leaving 2" unsewn in center of long edge.

3. Using needle, stitch pipe cleaner to each long side. Turn right side out. Stitch opening closed.

4. Cut out 3" x 4" rectangle. Fold each long side to center. Press flat. Wrap center of sewn rectangle, with raw edge to back of bow.

5. Fold raw edge under and stitch in place. Attach bow with floral wire.

GARLAND OF LOVE

Materials:

⅝"-wide green silk ribbon (20 yds.)

Premade fabric heart

Supplies:

Fabric scissors

H or G crochet hook

Instructions:

1. Chain-stitch first row to desired length.

2. Starting on second chain in from hook, make single crochet stitch, come up, pulling loop to desired length. Do not tighten loop but tighten crochet. Go to next stitch.

3. Repeat as needed.

Chain Stitch

1. Place slip knot on hook. With thumb and middle finger of left hand holding ribbon end, wrap ribbon up and over hook from back to front. *This movement* **(sts)** *is called yarn over* **(yo)** *and is basic to every crochet stitch.*

2. Use hook to pull ribbon through loop **(lp)** already on hook. *The ribbon combination of yo and pulling ribbon through lp makes one chain stitch* **(ch)**.

3. Repeat until desired length, trying to keep stitches even and relaxed, and sts same size. Hold ch near working area to keep it from twisting. Count sts as shown in diagram. (Do not count lp on hook or slip knot.)

Crochet Stitch

1. Insert hook under top two lps of second ch from hook and yo. Always work sts through top two lps of stitch unless directions specify otherwise.

2. Yo and pull ribbon though ch (two lps on hook).

3. Yo and pull ribbon through two lps on hook (one **(sc)** made).

Favors for wedding party members and guests can include items that are new or old, fancy or plain, sweet or sophisticated —it matters not. What is important is that they be sincere, personal, and chosen with the receiver in mind. The crackled cherub tile has a message written on the back to thank the recipient for not only everything they have done in regards to making this a perfect day . . . but for just being who they are—someone loved and appreciated.

CRACKLED CHERUB TILE

Materials:

4"-square wooden tile

Acrylic paints–gold,
antique white

Brass cherub charm

Brass corner charms (4)

Brown antiquing medium

Crackle medium

Craft glue

Supplies:

1" sponge brush

Paintbrush

Paper towels

Instructions:

1. Glue charms onto tile.

2. Paint entire tile with antique white paint.

3. Using sponge brush, apply crackle medium, following manufacturer's instructions.

4. Paint second coat with antique white paint.

5. Using sponge brush, apply antiquing medium over tile, following manufacturer's instructions. Using paper towels, remove excess antiquing medium.

6. Paint cherub with small amount of gold paint to highlight raised areas.

GLOWING CANDLE

Materials:

Candle

Glass dome

Iced window spray

Vase

Instructions:

1. Evenly spray glass dome with iced window spray, following manufacturer's instructions.

2. Turn glass dome over and place open side up in vase.

3. Place candle inside glass dome.

$\mathcal{G}$uests' Table

The wedding guests—those who are invited because of the sentimental times in days past that have been spent together. Those who are chosen to share this, the most memorable day of your young lives. Their table need also be a special place where thanks are given for the blessings shared, and the stories of moments lived long ago are told and retold. Their table should be set for those family and friends to enjoy good food, good conversation, and a wonderful day with just the right mixture of abandonment and restraint.

SITTING PRETTY

Materials:

Cotton fabric

Decoupage medium

Wrought-iron chair

Supplies:

1" sponge brush

Fabric scissors

Tape measure

Instructions:

See photograph on page 73.

1. Paint desired parts of chairs before decoupaging and wrapping chair.

2. Cut fabric into ½"–¾"-wide strips.

3. Apply decoupage medium to starting point on chair and top edge of one fabric strip. *The chair leg bottom is a good starting point.*

4. Place top edge of fabric at an angle onto decoupaged section of chair. Begin wrapping chair, making certain to overlap starting point. *Each successive wrap should overlap previous wrap.*

5. Repeat Steps 2–3, covering entire chair.

Materials:

Acrylic paints–lt. cream, charcoal gray, dk. pine green, tan

Buttons–assorted off-white, white

Crackle medium

Dried moss

Matte spray sealer

Oak gel stain

Unfinished wooden birdhouse

Supplies:

1" sponge brush

Flat paintbrush

Hot-glue gun

Paper towels

HONEYMOON COTTAGE

Instructions:

1. Paint walls of birdhouse with tan paint. Allow to dry. Apply second coat with tan paint.

2. Paint roof, eaves, and any trim with dk. pine green paint.

3. Paint steps and base of birdhouse with gray paint. Allow to dry.

4. Using sponge brush, apply crackle medium to walls, following manufacturer's instructions.

5. Paint walls of birdhouse with lt. cream paint. Allow to dry. *When paint is dry, write "Honeymoon Cottage" over door of birdhouse if desired.*

6. Using sponge brush, apply gel stain to entire birdhouse. Using paper towels, remove excess gel.

7. Spray with sealer.

8. Glue dried moss and buttons to roof as desired.

Materials:

1"-wide lace

Buttons–assorted white, specialty

Craft glue

Wooden heart-shaped box/hinged lid

Supplies:

Craft stick

Hot-glue gun

Tweezers

BUTTON-ADORNED BOX

Instructions:

1. Apply craft glue to top of box lid 2" at a time. Using tweezers and beginning at edges, place white buttons on glue. Allow to dry. *Make certain to leave hinge area free of glue.*

2. Glue lace onto sides of box and lid with craft glue.

3. Hot-glue specialty buttons onto center of lid.

4. Hot-glue additional buttons onto lace as desired.

BUTTON BOTTLE

Fill an attractive bottle such as an old cheese shaker with buttons. Glue scraps of lace and buttons onto the lid. How could an avid collector resist this charming way to display their collection?

Instructions:

1. With wrong side up, place paper on work surface. Roll lamp shade over paper to make certain it will cover properly.

2. Remove any fabric borders or decorations from lamp shade, making it is as smooth and flat as possible.

3. Spray outside of lamp shade with adhesive.

4. Place lamp shade on paper and firmly roll until lamp shade surface is covered, slightly overlapping edges.

5. Trim paper to lamp shade on side, adding 2"–3" at bottom and top.

6. Lightly spray underside of paper edges with adhesive. Wrap paper to inside of lamp shade.

PARCHMENT LAMP SHADE
Materials:

Oval or round lamp shade

Paper (to cover lamp shade)

Spray adhesive

Supplies:

Paper scissors

Pencil

It is wonderful to see what friends will do to make an evening the most memorable it can possibly be. Neighbors of Sara's Aunt Linda decorated the gazebo in the back of their home so that the view from her back porch was as lovely as the porch itself. It was a gift that will be remembered always by everyone.

SWEETHEART PILLOW

Materials:

10"-dia ecru Battenburg doily

10" pillow form

Antique brass cupid charms (4)

Coordinating thread

Ecru moiré faille fabric (½ yd.)

Embroidery flosses–blush, lt. brown, ecru, pale gold, ivory

Industrial-strength glue

Ribbons–9mm pale green (½ yd.), 9mm ivory (1 yd.), 2mm glitter-twill pale peach (2 yds.)

Silk ribbons–4mm pale green (3 yds.), 4mm ivory (2 yds.), 4mm off-white (2 yds.), 4mm taupe (2 yds.), 7mm ivory (1½ yds.), 7mm off-white (1 yd.), 7mm taupe (1½ yds.)

Small assorted laces (5–10)

Small pearl beads (18)

Supplies:

Fabric scissors

Iron/ironing board

Marking tool

Needles–sizes 20 & 22 chenille, size 7 embroidery, beading

Sewing machine

Instructions:

1. Cut 12" square from ecru moiré faille for pillow front. Center embroidery design on pillow front and mark location of heart shape.

2. Collage assorted laces onto pillow front up to outer edge of heart outline. Use finished or turned-under lace edge at heart outline. Overlap lace pieces ¼". Using sewing machine, stitch lace to pillow front with a narrow zigzag stitch, or stitch lace to pillow front with coordinating thread. Press.

3. See Transfer Sheet and Placement Diagram on page 84. Enlarge as indicated. Embroider design and assemble flower work, following Ribbon Embroidery and Flower Work Color and Stitch Guide on pages 82–83. Trim pillow front to 11" square. Cut 11" square from ecru moire faille for pillow back.

4. With right sides together, machine-stitch with ½" seam allowance, leaving one side open. Trim bulk from corners. Turn right side out. Insert pillow form. Slip-stitch opening closed.

5. With right side up, center and pin 10" doily underneath pillow. Slip-stitch doily to pillow back, up to pillow side seams.

6. Gather-stitch across pillow at 90° angle, ½" down from corner. See Diagram A. Gather corner. Repeat for all corners.

Diagram A

7. Cut 4mm ivory, off-white, taupe, and pale green silk ribbons into four 18" lengths each. Press if necessary. Layer set of four shades together. Tie small bow at center of layered lengths. Repeat for remaining three ribbon sets.

8. Stitch knot of bow to center of each puckered corner. Tie ribbon ends together, 4" from each bow. Trim ends to ½" below knot.

9. Glue brass cupids onto each corner of pillow.

Ribbon Embroidery and Flower Work Color and Stitch Guide

Silk ribbons listed below are 4mm unless otherwise indicated. Embroidery floss listed below is three strands unless otherwise indicated.

Step	Ribbon and Floss Color	Stitch and Flower Stitch
1. Girl's Body	Blush floss	Stem Stitch
2. Boy's Body	Ecru floss	Stem Stitch
3. Wings	Ivory floss	Stem Stitch
4. Girl's Hair	Ivory floss	Couching Stitch
5. Boy's Hair	Pale Gold floss	Couching Stitch
6. Facial Features	Lt. Brown floss	Couching Stitch
7. Girl's Tiara	Lt. Brown floss	Couching Stitch
8. Flower Stems	Lt. Brown floss	Couching Stitch
9. Flower Stems	Pale Gold floss	Couching Stitch
10. Rose Center	Ivory, 7mm	Ruffled Ribbon Stitch

Stitch center ruffle of each rose that is deeper in shade.

| 11. Rose Center | Off-White, 7mm | Ruffled Ribbon Stitch |

Stitch center ruffle of each rose that is palest in shade.

| 12. Outer Ruffle | Taupe, 7mm | Ruffled Ribbon Stitch |

Stitch outer ruffle of each rose that is deeper in shade. Stitch outer ruffle layer of a pale rose.

13. Textured Petals   Pale Peach Glitter–Twill, 2mm   Zigzag Runched Ribbon

Fray end of ribbon. Pull a center fiber to runched ribbon. Move gathers to meet fabric. Stitch into fabric at end of gathers to secure. Stitch small sprays, full circles and half-circles. Tack with matching thread to shape stitches.

14. Large Leaves   Pale Green, 9mm   Loop Petal Stitch Variation

Use larger chenille needle.

15. Medium Leaves   Ivory, 9mm   Loop Petal Stitch Variation

Use larger chenille needle.

16. Small Leaves   Pale Green, 9mm   Ribbon Stitch

Tack center of ivory leaves with pale green leaves. Add additional pale green leaves around heart.

17. Bouquet   Ivory, 7mm   French Knot

Stitch very loose French knots for flowers in bouquet.

18. Bouquet   Off–White, 7mm   French Knot

Stitch very loose French knots.

19. Bouquet   Taupe, 7mm   French Knot

20. Bouquet Leaves   Pale Green, 4mm   Ribbon Stitch

21. Beads   Pearls   Beading Stitch

Using beading needle, stitch pearls where shown. A variety of sizes can be used if desired.

22. Bow   Pale Peach Glitter–Twill, 2mm

Cut 15" length of ribbon. Tie bow near center. Stitch knot of bow to bouquet. Tack bow loops lightly. Tie knots in ribbon ends. Drape and tack knots.

Beading Stitch

1. Using doubled thread, bring needle up at A. Slide bead on needle and go down at B.

2. Knot thread.

B A

Couching Stitch

1. Complete a straight-stitch base by bringing needle up at A and going down at B. *Keep ribbon flat and loose.*

2. Make a short, tight straight stitch across ribbon base to "couch" straight stitch. Come up at C on one side of ribbon. Go down at D on opposite side of ribbon. *This will cause ribbon to gather and pucker. The straight-stitch base is tacked at varying intervals.*

3. Repeat as needed to fill desired area.

French Knot

1. Bring needle up at A, smoothly wrap ribbon once around needle.

2. Hold ribbon securely off to one side and go down at B.

3. Repeat as needed to fill desired area.

Placement Diagram

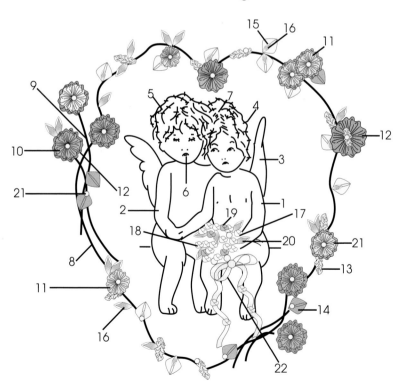

84

Loop Petal Stitch

1. Bring needle up at A. Form small loop and go down at B, piercing ribbon.

2. Tack down center of stitches with matching color of floss (1 strand).

3. Repeat as needed to fill desired area.

Ribbon Stitch

1. Come up through fabric at A. Lay ribbon flat on fabric. At end of stitch, pierce ribbon with needle. Slowly pull length of ribbon through to back, allowing ends of ribbon to curl.

Ruffled Ribbon Stitch

1. Knot one end of ribbon. Bring needle up at A. Using needle, separate one strong thread from selvage of ribbon.

2. Pull thread to gather ribbon to desired length. Bring needle down through fabric at B. Tack ribbon to wrong side of stitching. *Make a series of ruffled Ribbon Stitches to appear as one.*

3. Repeat as needed to fill desired area.

Stem Stitch

1. Bring needle up at A. Keep ribbon to left and below needle.

2. Go down at B and back up at C.

3. Repeat as needed to fill desired area.

Zigzag Runched Ribbon

1. Starting ½" from one end, mark ¾"-wide intervals for total of 13 intervals on one selvage edge and 12 on opposite edge. Gather-stitch, connecting dots in zigzag fashion. Pull gathers and secure thread.

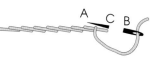

2. Repeat as needed to fill desired area.

$\mathcal{G}$uests' Table

Each guest table can be decorated differently, which allows for the use of those treasured items that are borrowed from those who know you best.

CUPCAKE BOXES

Materials (for one box):

4"-square lace

6"-square heavy-weight cardboard

8"-square lightweight cardboard

Decorative trim (1¾ yds.)

Fabric: 8" x 18"

Polyester stuffing

Tacky craft glue

Supplies (for both boxes):

½"-dia wooden dowel

Craft scissors

Fabric scissors

Masking tape

Paint roller

Pencil

Photocopy machine

Sewing needle

Instructions (for one box):

1. Photocopy patterns on pages 88–89, enlarging as indicated. Trace patterns onto appropriate cardboard and fabric as indicated. Cut out cardboard and fabric pieces as indicated.

2. Roll glue onto paint roller. Completely cover roller's surface, then roll off extra glue in dish. Paint entire surface of one side of OUTSIDE BOX SIDE cardboard with glue.

3. Place glued cardboard onto wrong side of corresponding fabric and press in place.

4. Turn fabric and cardboard over and smooth fabric completely, eliminating any wrinkles immediately. *Fabric should adhere to cardboard everywhere, especially at the edges.*

5. Turn laminated cardboard wrong side up. Use paint roller to paint edge of cardboard and fabric with glue. Trim bulk from each corner, then wrap extended fabric over onto glued edges.

6. Double-check corners for fraying fabric, daubing frays with glue and wrap as necessary. Allow to dry.

7. Repeat Steps 2–6 for OUTSIDE BOX SIDE, INSIDE BOX SIDE, INSIDE BOTTOM, INSIDE LID, and BASE.

8. Place OUTSIDE BOX SIDE wrong side up on work surface. Beginning

Enlarge 200%

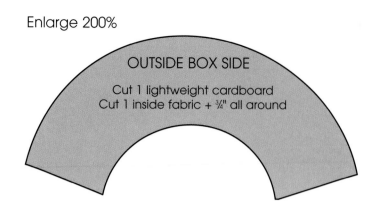

OUTSIDE BOX SIDE
Cut 1 lightweight cardboard
Cut 1 inside fabric + ¾" all around

Enlarge 200%

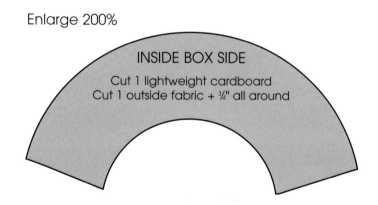

INSIDE BOX SIDE
Cut 1 lightweight cardboard
Cut 1 outside fabric + ¾" all around

at outer short edge, carefully roll with ½" dowel. *Because box has cone shape, change dowel placement to match flair of box as necessary.* Place INSIDE BOX SIDE right side up on work surface and repeat process.

9. Adjoin short edges of INSIDE BOX SIDE and secure with masking tape. Working with box upside down, slip INSIDE BOTTOM with wrong side toward bottom of box into assembled INSIDE BOX SIDE. Secure with thin bead of glue and hold until glue dries.

Enlarge 125%

LID and INSIDE LID

Cut 2 heavy-weight cardboard
Cut 1 outer fabric + ½" all around
Cut 1 inside fabric + ½" all around

Enlarge 125%

BASE

Cut 1 heavy-weight
cardboard
Cut 1 outer fabric +
½" all around

Enlarge 125%

INSIDE BOTTOM

Cut 1 heavy-weight
cardboard
Cut 1 inside fabric +
½" all around

10. Glue edge of trim onto wrong side top edge of INSIDE BOX SIDE. Cover wrong side of INSIDE BOX SIDE with a thin layer of thin-bodied tacky glue. With wrong sides together, wrap OUTSIDE BOX SIDE around INSIDE BOX SIDE, aligning top edges. Press together and hold until INSIDE BOX SIDE has bonded to OUTSIDE BOX SIDE.

11. Turn box upside down. Glue edge of trim onto underside edge around bottom of box. Glue wrong side of BASE onto bottom of box.

12. Section and mark LID and lid fabric into quarters. Glue edge of lid fabric to wrong side edge of LID, matching marks. Ease fabric in between marks to fit LID. Leave one section unglued. Firmly fill with stuffing. Glue remaining section to underside of LID. Overlay lid fabric with lace and glue edge of lace to underside edge of LID.

13. Glue edge of trim onto wrong side edge of LID. With wrong sides together, glue LID to INSIDE LID.

14. Embellish lid top as desired.

CHINA PLATE

A plate or glass memento can be personalized with a message from the wedding party by using pens made for writing on china. Plates or glass mementos are handwashable after curing for several days.

Buffet Table

There is no prettier way to serve your wedding guests on a beautiful summer afternoon than with scoops of handmade ice cream. Each is flavored with fresh fruit and topped with large lollipops that bring back happy summer days long since past. Even the younger guests will sit quietly to eat these desserts that are part of the wedding feast. All of the table decorations here are bold and oversized. The flowers made from wallpaper are bunched into a garden can and ceramic garden pots are filled with the fruits of the season.

Bohemian Chic

EVERY bride should have the wedding she has always dreamed of. A ceremony with the words, "from this day forward . . . ." because these are words of promise. Wondrous words that are filled with the hope of a thousand tomorrow's. A dress that is as delicate as the breeze that causes the autumn leaves to fall on a September afternoon. Decorations that are vibrant with color and texture and awash with light. A wedding that is unexpected, uniquely her own, and never forgotten. Beth had always imagined just such a time and a place filled with such color and surprise. On the appointed day, she was married to James in just this way. Hers was a Bohemian wedding. Chic, stylish, and filled with the colors of autumn. There was beaded fringe on the brocade tablecloths, the guests were served small cupcakes with wild red roses on brightly printed paper plates. Tassels and beaded glass vases hung from the vibrant gold umbrella of the guest book table and each family member and friend was given handmade bubble blowers to send the couple on their way. It was a day woven with magic—just her way.

Book Table

On the guest book table is a scrapbook designed by Jill Schwartz from Elements that is being used not only for guests to sign their name, but to leave a wish for the bride and groom and have pictures, taken at the wedding, added at a later date. It, too, is an individual way of observing tradition.

BEJEWELED TABLE RUNNER

Materials:

20" x 54" fabric

Beaded fringe (1 yd.)

Canvas tape

Iron-on webbing (optional)

Supplies:

Fabric scissors

Sewing machine

Instructions:

Fabric should have finished edges before beginning.

1. Blind-stitch 1" hem along side edges of fabric. *Iron-on webbing can be used.*

2. Cut beaded fringe in half. Stitch canvas tape to beaded fringe lengths.

3. Fold canvas tape under runner and finger-press, making certain canvas tape does not show.

4. Stitch raw edges under runner.

TREASURE BOX

Materials:

Acrylic paints–black, blue, brown, gold, green, red, white

Crackle medium

Gesso

Gloss varnish

Objects d'art–beads, knobs, miniature animals, tiny salt shakers

Wood glue (optional)

Wooden box

Wooden trim medallion (optional)

Supplies:

#6 paintbrush

1" sponge brush

Clean rags

Hot-glue gun

Pencil

Transfer paper

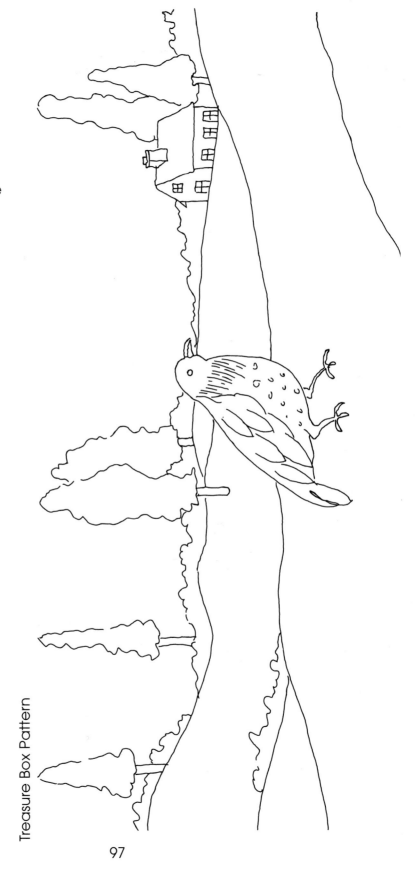

Treasure Box Pattern

97

Instructions:

If using wooden medallion trim, glue to top of lid with wood glue.

1. Using sponge brush, paint box and lid with mixture of five parts gesso to two parts gold paint. Allow to dry.

2. Draw background onto box front and sides. See photograph on page 96.

3. Using transfer paper and pencil, transfer Treasure Box Pattern and Treasure Box Side Pattern on pages 97–98 onto box. See photograph. *Tracing may need to be enlarged or reduced depending on size of box.*

4. Paint lid top and edge with green paint. Allow to dry.

5. Paint sky on box with blue paint. Allow to dry.

6. Paint lower hills with mixture of two parts brown paint to five parts gold paint. Allow to dry.

7. Paint treetops and grass at bird's feet with green paint. Allow to dry.

8. Wash roof with red paint. Allow to dry.

9. Paint tree trunks with brown paint. Allow to dry.

Treasure Box Side Pattern

10. Wash bird with brown paint.

11. Paint chimney and bird's back feather with brown paint. Allow to dry.

12. Paint Vs on breast and stomach of bird with mixture of green and brown paints.

13. Paint eye, beak, and windows with black paint. Allow to dry.

14. Dot bird's eye with white paint for highlight. Allow to dry.

15. Using sponge brush, apply crackle medium to box, following manufacturer's instructions. Allow to dry.

16. Apply varnish over crackle. Allow to dry.

17. Hot-glue object d'art onto top of lid.

Instructions:

1. Apply leafing adhesive to top of decanter and stopper, following manufacturer's instructions.

2. Apply gold leafing to top of decanter and stopper, following manufacturer's instructions.

These fanciful rose holders, which are hung wherever guests might be, are made by Poco A Poco Imports, but could be the inspiration for tiny cups and vases that are collected from family and friends and hung by strung beads in the garden with flowers or candles.

GOLD-TOPPED DECANTER

Materials:

Decorative glass decanter

Gold leafing sheets

Leafing adhesive

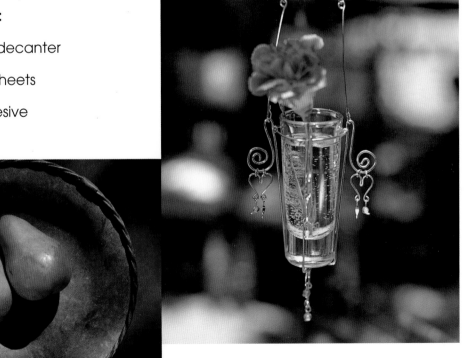

Bride's & Groom's Table

The bride's and groom's table at a Bohemian Chic wedding is one of intrigue and wonder. The glass plates are actually green Christmas dishes borrowed from a cousin, the napkin rings are bracelets that were purchased at a discount store, the intricate blue box was handmade by the bride's mother and holds a wish for the bride and groom from the parents, and the "frame" is a business card holder. The wine glasses for toasting are a gift from the best man and are handblown in deep rich colors, and the favors on the plates are satin beaded hearts made by the bridesmaids, filled with good luck charms and tokens. The dilapidated elegance of the weathered table reminds the guests of an old Spanish villa and the brocade tablecloth has the vibrant charm of a Moroccan celebration.

This is a wedding whose decorations, guests, and honored couple are as contemporary as they are traditional, as extravagant as they are conservative, and as enthusiastic as they are contemplative. They are a couple in love with tradition . . . not bound by it.

PARASOL EMBELLISHMENT

Materials:

⅛"-wide matching cording (4 yds.)

1" unfinished wooden wheels (12)

3" tassels

6" floral wire

Acrylic paints–lt. green, tangerine, violet, lt. yellow

Glossy spray sealer

Unfinished wooden beads–12mm (12), 16mm (12), 1"-dia. (12)

Supplies:

Assorted paintbrushes

Craft scissors

Metallic gold paint marker

Instructions:

1. Paint beads and wheels with desired paint colors (except tangerine). Allow to dry. Using metallic marker, draw designs on violet painted beads.

2. See Dry-brush on page 119. Dry-brush yellow bead with tangerine paint.

3. Cut cording into 12" lengths. Place cording in loop at top of tassel. Center cording in loop.

4. Fold 6" piece of wire around cording, about 1½" from raw ends. *Wire will serve as needle to thread the beads onto the tassel.*

5. Thread wheel, large bead, medium bead, and small bead onto tassel.

6. Knot cording by small bead. Tie another knot toward end of cording. Trim ends if necessary.

The heart-shaped favors placed on the bride's and groom's plates are each different. They were made by the bridesmaids and are filled with good luck charms and tokens. The napkin rings are bracelets that were purchased at discount stores and the blue box holds a wish from the parents for the bride and groom.

BLUE EMBELLISHED BOX

Materials:

Assorted beads

Assorted seashells

Blue acrylic paint

Box/lid

Craft glue

Wood varnish

103

Supplies:

#6 paintbrush

1" sponge brush

Instructions:

1. Paint entire box with blue paint. Allow to dry.

2. Using sponge brush, apply varnish to painted box, following manufacturer's instructions.

3. Working in one small area at a time, apply glue to top and sides of lid.

4. Press shells and beads into glue.

PATCHWORK PORCELAIN FAVORS

Materials (for satin lid):

½"-dia. brass button

3" round black porcelain jar/lid for needle work

4" x 4" unbleached muslin

Assorted bugle beads

Assorted colored satin fabrics (scraps) (7)

Assorted seed beads

Embroidery flosses (to match three satin fabrics)

Supplies:

Dressmaker's pen

Embroidery needle

Fabric scissors

Instructions:

1. Center and trace acetate circle from jar onto muslin. It may be useful to trace the circle again after some or all of fabric pieces are placed.

2. Begin layering fabrics by pinning one piece to muslin. Layer second and third pieces over edges of first at varying angles. Fold under ⅛" seam allowances on edges that overlap first piece. Slip-stitch folded edges with matching floss. Complete with four remaining fabrics. See photograph at right.

3. Embellish seam lines with embroidery stitches. Add button and beads.

4. Cut muslin on pen line.

5. Assemble lid, following manufacturer's instructions.

*P*arents' Table

The parents' table also has napkin rings that are dime-store bracelets, but the tiny porcelain jars with the handmade lids are filled with tiny gifts from the bride and groom. Each parent receives one and each is different—one has buttons from the bride's christening dress.

PATCHWORK PORCELAIN FAVORS

Materials (for ribbon lid):

³⁄₁₆"-dia. faceted metal beads (3)

½"-dia. metal button

3" round black porcelain jar /lid for needlework

3"-wide assorted colored ribbons (4)

4" x 4" unbleached muslin

Matching threads (for ribbons)

Supplies:

Dressmaker's pen

Fabric scissors

Sewing needle

Instructions:

1. Center and trace acetate circle from jar onto muslin. *It may be useful to trace the circle again after some or all of fabric pieces are placed.*

2. Arrange ribbon in layers as desired. Tack ribbon edges to muslin. Stitch button and beads to ribbons.

3. Cut muslin on pen line.

4. Assemble lid, following manufacturer's instructions.

MARBLED CHAIRS

Materials:

Acrylic paints–dk. blue, burgundy, metallic gold, off-white, white

Clear mixing glaze

High-gloss water-based varnish

Wooden chair

Supplies:

½" flat China-bristle paintbrush

½" flat soft-bristle paintbrush

#0 liner paintbrush

Craft sticks

Disposable plates

Natural sponge

Newspaper

Softening paintbrush

Continued on page 108.

Continued from page 106.

Instructions:

1. Prepare chairs. *Wood furniture which is new and unfinished, and is going to be entirely covered with paint, generally requires a single coat of primer. Old furniture which has been previously stained, painted, or varnished is best stripped with chemical stripping agent or painted with the appropriate primer.*

2. Using soft-bristle paint brush, apply base coat with off-white paint to chairs where marbling finish is to be applied. Allow to dry.

3. Using craft stick and disposable plate, mix two parts mixing glaze with one part white paint. Mix well.

4. Thoroughly wet and wring out sponge.

5. Sponge chair with mixing glaze/paint mixture, then lightly blot off excess onto newspaper.

6. Using gentle pressure, sponge over surface of chair in a random pattern, slightly rotating your hand each time. Lift and repeat several times. Rinse sponge and repeat. *Overlap rotations so they blend into a natural-looking pattern.*

7. Using craft stick and disposable plate, mix two parts mixing glaze with one part dark blue paint.

8. Sponge over mixing glaze/white areas. Leave patches of white paint exposed.

9. Using craft stick and disposable plate, mix two parts mixing glaze with one part metallic paint.

10. Sponge over mixing glaze/dk. blue areas. Leave patches of each color exposed. Allow to dry.

11. Using #0 liner paintbrush, drag a burgundy paint line across surface to create "veins."

12. Using softening paintbrush, gently brush across wet veins.

13. Using ½" China-bristle paintbrush, apply generous coat of water-based varnish to chairs to seal. Allow to dry for 24 hours. Apply second coat and allow to dry.

Guests' Table

One might find the guests of a garden Bohemian Chic wedding taking their wine and cheese on the hand-dyed shawls that are scattered through the gardens. The colors of the fabrics and the flowers brighten the mood and lift the soul. They are bright and fresh, and welcome a new life together.

Guests' Table

Flowers do not have to be fresh in order to bring forth the colors of nature. These are beaded and each one can be made by a family member. The array of different flower types, shapes, and colors will be amazing and at the end of the reception the flowers can be gathered together and given to the bride and groom as a housewarming gift—one that will never fade and grow old. They will always be as beautiful and treasured as they were on their wedding day.

Deeply colored paper plates are so beautiful and yet so practical and economical. A special golden touch is added for each guest with a gold-lacquered fortune cookie, containing a wish from the bride and groom.

JEWELED ROSE

Instructions:

The long-stemmed Jeweled Rose is formed with individual petals in three layers of graduated sizes.

1. Apply layer of tacky white glue onto button. Allow to set for one minute.

2. Working over mixing tray, pour gold beads near bottom edge of button. Pour sunset red beads onto center portion of button. Pour lt. pink beads onto top of button. Press beads against glue. Pour off excess beads. Allow to dry.

3. Apply decoupage medium to button.

Materials:

14-gauge copper wire

26-gauge gold wire

¾"-dia gold button

11/0 seed beads—gold (two containers),
lt. green (two containers),
dk. red (two containers),
tangerine (two containers)

8/0 seed beads—lt. pink
(two containers)

Supplies:

Decoupage medium

Glue brush

Mixing trays (2)

Needle-nosed pliers

Tacky craft glue

Wire cutters

4. For top flower layer, cut six 20" pieces from gold wire.

5. Trim 8" from one 20" piece of wire and set aside. Slide 52 seed beads onto remaining 12" piece of wire, beginning and ending with dk. red beads and using gold and tangerine beads together randomly. Slide beads toward middle of wire. Bend wire to form loop and twist ends together just below first and last bead.

6. Tightly wrap one end of 8" piece of wire around top of loop. Trim end flush to beads. Slide 20 gold and tangerine seed beads onto wire, shading beads from light to dark. Extend wire to bottom of loop, so that beaded wire lays straight within center of loop. Twist wires together. Trim 4" from wire.

7. Tightly wrap one end of 4" piece of wire near top of loop, about three beads to left of center wire. Slide 17 gold and tangerine beads seed beads onto wire, shading beads from light to dark. Wrap wire around center wire, three beads up from bottom of center wire. Slide another 17 beads onto wire, shading beads from dark to light. Extend wire to loop top. Tightly wrap wire around top of loop, about three beads to right of center wire. Trim wire ends flush to beads at top of loop.

8. Repeat Steps 5–7 to make six flower petals. Twist six petals together to form top flower layer.

9. For middle flower layer, cut six 20" pieces from gold wire.

10. Trim 8" from one 20" piece of wire and set aside. Slide 60 seed beads onto remaining 12" piece of wire, and continue as in Step 5. Repeat Steps 6–7 to make six petals of this size.

11. Twist six petals together to form middle flower layer. Slip top layer's wires through center of middle layer. Twist wires together.

12. For bottom flower layer, cut six 20" pieces from gold wire.

13. Trim 8" from one 20" piece and set aside. Slide 72 gold and tangerine beads seed beads onto remaining 12" piece of wire, and continue as in Step 4. Repeat Steps 6–7 with 23 beads for center wire and 20 beads for each side wire to make six petals of this size.

14. Twist six petals together to form bottom flower layer. Slip top and middle layer's wires through center of bottom layer. Twist wires together.

15. Cut two 10" pieces from gold wire. Slide wires through button shaft. Twist wires together beneath button, so button is not floppy. Slide button wires through center of flower layers. Twist wires together.

16. Cut one 18" piece from copper wire. Using needle-nosed pliers, bend small loop at one end of wire. Tightly wire flower layers to copper wire through loop, creating flower stem.

17. Cut two 18" pieces from copper wire. Using needle-nosed pliers, bend small loop at one end of one wire. Place all copper wires

together, with loops of wires at opposite ends. Wrap combined copper wires with gold wire, creating thick sturdy flower stem.

18. For leaves, cut two 20" pieces from gold wire.

19. Slide 112 lt. green beads onto one wire. Slide beads toward center of wire. Bend wire to form loop and twist ends together just below first and last bead.

20. Tightly wrap one end of remaining 20" wire around top of loop. Trim end flush to beads. Slide 50 lt. green beads onto wire. Extend wire to bottom of loop, so that beaded wire lays straight within center of loop. Twist wires together. *Do not trim wire at this point.*

21. Cut one 15" piece from gold wire. Tightly wrap one end of wire near top of loop, about two beads to left of center wire. Slide 47 beads onto wire. Wrap wire around center wire, four beads up from bottom of center wire. Slide another 47 beads onto wire. Extend wire and tightly wrap wire around top of loop, about two beads to right of center wire. Trim wire ends flush to beads.

22. Cut one 7" piece from gold wire. Tightly wrap one end of wire near top of loop, two beads to left of previous wire. Wrap wire around side of loop, five beads from loop bottom. Trim wire ends flush to beads.

23. Working with center wire, slide lt. green seed beads onto wire for 3" length. Tightly wrap beaded wire around remaining wires to create 1½" long leaf stem. Wire leaf stem onto flower stem.

24. Repeat Steps 19–23 to make second leaf.

25. Cut one 90" piece of gold wire. Attach wire to underside of flower. Slide lt. green seed beads onto wire for a 3" length. Tightly wrap beaded wire around flower stem, then slide beads onto wire for another 3". Wrap around flower stem. Continue in this manner to cover length of flower stem. Wrap wire several times through loop at bottom of flower stem to secure.

When a wedding is as beautiful as a bride's dreams, when tender touches and gestures abound, when there is an appreciation for the unusual, then this is when the memories will be the jewels that are truly treasured.

Serving Table

Wouldn't it be wonderful to have a fairy godmother sweep down and make everything perfect? Family and friends attending such a grand Bohemian Chic wedding celebration might begin to think she had. For this is the place where the unusual has been used. Sunflower yellow pitchers are used to hold cherries, the cupcakes are decorated with rich red roses and placed on a handmade cake plate, the guests are invited to take a bubble blower for the couple's departure, and the decorations are gathered from nature. It is here that a rusted garden urn holds shells collected from family vacations to the beach. Every detail is recognized, every piece is collected, and nothing but the wedding vows are new.

PAINTED CAKE STAND

Materials:

16"-dia. unfinished wooden plate

Acrylic paints–dk. brown, metallic gold, lt. green, peach, plum, tangerine, violet, wine, lt. yellow

Construction adhesive

Glossy spray sealer

Old lamp base

Wooden disc with hole (to cover upper lamp bolt)

Supplies:

Assorted paintbrushes

Craft knife

Extrafine sanding pads

Toothpick

Instructions:

1. Remove electrical elements such as cord and harp from lamp. Fasten lamp back together.

2. Slip wooden discover bolt on lamp base, using craft knife enlarge hole if necessary. Apply glue to disc to secure in place. Allow glue to dry for several hours.

3. Lightly sand lamp base.

4. Paint lamp base with lt. green, wine, and lt. yellow paints. See photograph on facing page. Allow paint to dry and, if necessary, reapply paint until color is even.

5. Dry-brush lamp base with tangerine paint.

6. Mix plum paint with a little water. Paint six flowers by creating petals in a rough teardrop shape with plum paint mixture. Allow to dry.

7. Stipple around edges with peach paint.

8. Stipple a rough circle in center of each flower with dk. brown paint.

9. Create two to three leaves on the edge of each flower with lt. green paint.

10. Stipple edge of flowers with violet paint.

11. Dip toothpick into metallic gold paint and dot center of flower.

12. Base-coat plate with lt. yellow paint. Allow to dry. Lightly sand plate. Apply second coat lt. yellow paint to plate.

13. Paint wide stripes on outside edge of plate with wine paint.

14. Paint ½" ring 2" from edge of plate with lt. green paint.

15. Dry-brush stripes and edge of plate with tangerine paint.

16. Make flowers as in Step 6 on several yellow stripes.

17. Apply glue to disc, then center and press plate on disc. Allow glue to set up. Spray cake stand with sealer.

Dry-brush

Dry-brushing is used to apply color and shadows.

1. Dip paintbrush into paint, then rub paintbrush back and forth on palette to distribute paint into paintbrush.

2. Rub paintbrush on paper towel or old rag to remove excess paint. When paint begins to have powder-like look, apply paint to project.

Stipple

1. Dip paintbrush into paint, daub tip of paintbrush on paper towel to remove excess paint.

2. Using pouncing motion, apply paint lightly to project.

$\mathcal{R}$eception Table

One much honored tradition, regardless of the wedding style, is the giving and displaying of gifts. The giving of gifts should be as honored as the giver of the gift, and to do so, a special place should be designated on which to set and display all gifts given. Here, the first gift is the shoes that were worn by the bride when she was a flower girl long ago. They are as precious to her today as they will be tomorrow and were on the day she wore them.

FLOWER-GIRL SHOES

Materials:

¼"-wide elastic (7"–8")

1½"-wide wire-edged ribbon (26")

7" x 13" tulle

Cotton fabric for lining (scraps)

Crocheted lace (scraps)

Interfacing (scraps)

Matching thread

Plush knit for sole lining (scraps)

Purchased rosette (2)

Satin fabric for shoes (scraps)

Thick brushed felt for soles (scraps)

Supplies:

Photocopy machine

Scissors–craft, fabric

Sewing needle

Sewing machine

Straight pins

Instructions:

Allow ¼" for seam allowances.

1. Photocopy shoe patterns on page 124. Enlarging or decreasing as needed. *Make certain the foot fits inside the dotted stitching line before cutting out the fabric to make shoe. Cut out patterns. Trace patterns onto appropriate fabrics.*

2. Cut out all shoe pieces, including lining and interfacing. Using sewing machine, baste-stitch interfacing to wrong side of

UPPER SHOE pieces. See Diagram A. *You may want to zigzag-stitch around the edges to prevent fraying. Stitch scraps of lace to embellish toe ends.*

Diagram A

3. With right sides together, stitch UPPER SHOE and UPPER SHOE LINING together, along inner curved edge. Clip curves, turn right side out and press.

4. With right sides together, stitch SHOE BACK and SHOE BACK LINING together along upper edge. Turn right side out and press toward SHOE BACK.

5. Open out UPPER SHOE and lining with right sides together, stitch SHOE BACK to UPPER SHOE pieces. Cut elastic in half. Zigzag-stitch elastic ¼" below seam to wrong side of SHOE BACK LINING, stretching elastic as you stitch. See Diagram B.

Diagram B

6. With right sides together, stitch SHOE BACK to UPPER SHOE pieces, matching seams. Repeat for remaining side of shoe, until entire UPPER SHOE is connected. Baste-stitch all raw edges together. See Diagram C.

Diagram C

7. Pin shoe together as follows: SOLE LINING with right side facing up. See Diagram D. Place shoe on top of SOLE

Diagram D

so UPPER SHOE LINING is next to right side of SOLE. Pin SOLE to UPPER SHOE, so right sides

face each other. Pin all layers to each other, starting at pointed toe and working around each side of shoe, tucking shoe inside SOLE and SOLE LINING as you pin. Baste-stitch edges together, leaving 2" of back part of shoe open. Clip inward ¼" on each side where stitching ends.

8. Stitch shoe, trim excess seam allowance, and turn shoe so lining side is out.

9. Pin open ends of heel together and baste-stitch, easing in fullness. Machine-stitch. Zigzag-stitch raw edges. Turn shoe right side out and stitch on trims as desired. See Diagram E.

Diagram E

10. Cut two 3½" x 13" pieces of tulle. Gather-stitch tulle lengthwise down the center. Pull gather tight, creating pom-pom. Stitch pom-pom to front of shoe. Trim tulle to 1¼" from center.

11. Tack rosette to center of pom-pom.

SOLE
Cut 2
Cut 2 linings

SHOE BACK
Cut 2
Cut 2 linings

UPPER SHOE
Cut 2
Cut 2 linings
Cut 2 interfacing

124

TWIG TOPIARY

Materials:

6" x 45" taupe tulle (2)

Dried berries, dried garland, dried juniper, dried lemon leaves, dried pods

Dried moss (to cover plant container base)

Fabric (to cover plant container)

Floral foam (to fill container)

Matte acrylic sealer

Plant container

Twig topiary form (22")

Supplies:

Craft scissors

Floral wire

Hot-glue gun

Iron/ironing board

Instructions:

1. Iron fabric. With wrong side of fabric up, place plant container in middle of fabric. Bring ends up around container and tuck ends inside container.

2. Cut floral foam into small pieces and mound foam in container, making it higher in the center.

3. Center and push twig base into foam. *The twig may be crooked, but this gives the finished piece its charm.*

4. Beginning at top of topiary, wrap with dried garland and moss. Hot-glue as necessary.

5. Beginning at top of topiary, wind one piece of tulle down topiary. Tuck end of tulle into garland. Hot-glue into place as necessary.

6. Hot-glue lemon leaves onto base, in a variety of directions. Step back from topiary and check for even coverage. Adjust as necessary.

7. Hot-glue juniper then fern leaves, tucking them under lemon leaves or tulle as desired.

8. Hot-glue dried flowers and pods as desired.

9. Mound moss around base of twig stem. Hot-glue as necessary.

10. Tie bow around top of container with remaining tulle. Trim ends of bow in an inverted V-shape.

126

CONVERSION CHART
mm-millimeters cm-centimeters
inches to millimeters and centimeters

inches	mm	cm	inches	cm	inches	cm
1/8	3	0.3	9	22.9	30	76.2
1/4	6	0.6	10	25.4	31	78.7
3/8	10	1.0	11	27.9	32	81.3
1/2	13	1.3	12	30.5	33	83.8
5/8	16	1.6	13	33.0	34	86.4
3/4	19	1.9	14	35.6	35	88.9
7/8	22	2.2	15	38.1	36	91.4
1	25	2.5	16	40.6	37	94.0
1 1/4	32	3.2	17	43.2	38	96.5
1 1/2	38	3.8	18	45.7	39	99.1
1 3/4	44	4.4	19	48.3	40	101.6
2	51	5.1	20	50.8	41	104.1
2 1/2	64	6.4	21	53.3	42	106.7
3	76	7.6	22	55.9	43	109.2
3 1/2	89	8.9	23	58.4	44	111.8
4	102	10.2	24	61.0	45	114.3
4 1/2	114	11.4	25	63.5	46	116.8
5	127	12.7	26	66.0	47	119.4
6	152	15.2	27	68.6	48	121.9
7	178	17.8	28	71.1	49	124.5
8	203	20.3	29	73.7	50	127.0

yards to meters

yards	meters	yards	meters	yards	meters	yards	meters	yards	meters
1/8	0.11	2 1/8	1.94	4 1/8	3.77	6 1/8	5.60	8 1/8	7.43
1/4	0.23	2 1/4	2.06	4 1/4	3.89	6 1/4	5.72	8 1/4	7.54
3/8	0.34	2 3/8	2.17	4 3/8	4.00	6 3/8	5.83	8 3/8	7.66
1/2	0.46	2 1/2	2.29	4 1/2	4.11	6 1/2	5.94	8 1/2	7.77
5/8	0.57	2 5/8	2.40	4 5/8	4.23	6 5/8	6.06	8 5/8	7.89
3/4	0.69	2 3/4	2.51	4 3/4	4.34	6 3/4	6.17	8 3/4	8.00
7/8	0.80	2 7/8	2.63	4 7/8	4.46	6 7/8	6.29	8 7/8	8.12
1	0.91	3	2.74	5	4.57	7	6.40	9	8.23
1 1/8	1.03	3 1/8	2.86	5 1/8	4.69	7 1/8	6.52	9 1/8	8.34
1 1/4	1.14	3 1/4	2.97	5 1/4	4.80	7 1/4	6.63	9 1/4	8.46
1 3/8	1.26	3 3/8	3.09	5 3/8	4.91	7 3/8	6.74	9 3/8	8.57
1 1/2	1.37	3 1/2	3.20	5 1/2	5.03	7 1/2	6.86	9 1/2	8.69
1 5/8	1.49	3 5/8	3.31	5 5/8	5.14	7 5/8	6.97	9 5/8	8.80
1 3/4	1.60	3 3/4	3.43	5 3/4	5.26	7 3/4	7.09	9 3/4	8.92
1 7/8	1.71	3 7/8	3.54	5 7/8	5.37	7 7/8	7.20	9 7/8	9.03
2	1.83	4	3.66	6	5.49	8	7.32	10	9.14

INDEX